# Best
# STO

# THE HOLIDAY THAT WENT WRONG

*Jennifer Rees Larcombe*

Illustrated by Steve Björkman

Marshall Pickering
*An Imprint of HarperCollinsPublishers*

Marshall Pickering is an Imprint of
HarperCollins*Religious*
Part of HarperCollins*Publishers*
77–85 Fulham Palace Road,
London W6 8JB
www.christian-publishing.co.uk

First published in 1992 in Great Britain
by Marshall Pickering as part of the
*Children's Bible Story Book* by Jennifer Rees Larcombe
This edition published in 2000 by Marshall Pickering

1 3 5 7 9 10 8 6 4 2

Text copyright © 1992, 2000 Jennifer Rees Larcombe
Illustrations copyright © 2000 Steve Björkman

Jennifer Rees Larcombe and Steve Björkman assert the moral right to be
identified as the author and illustrator of this work.

A catalogue record for this book is
available from the British Library.

ISBN 0 551 03249 9

Printed and bound in Hong Kong

# THE HOLIDAY THAT WENT WRONG

One day some men brought Jesus **terrible news.** 'King Herod has killed your cousin John.' For months poor John had been shut in a **dungeon** because he had told the King and Queen just how bad they were.
Now they had **cut off his head.**

Jesus felt so **sad** he

# longed to be alone for a while.

'We all need a holiday,' he said to his disciples.
'You look tired. Let's row over to the other side
of the lake and find a **really lonely** place to
camp.'

As the boat skimmed over the water, leaving the crowds far behind, they all began to feel better. 'No more people pushing round us,' laughed Peter as the boat crunched on a sandy shore. 'This place is

just right for a holiday.

Nothing but grass and birds.'

They hardly had time to build their camp fire before they were **groaning** in dismay. **Surging** towards them along the beach came the crowds. They must have seen Jesus slip away, and **thousands** of them had **dashed** round the lakeside to catch up with him.

One of the first to arrive was a little boy. He had been **walking for hours** because he was so desperate to see Jesus.

He **hadn't even had time to eat** the food his mother had packed for his journey.

'Oh **no**!' grumbled Peter. 'Send them away, Lord.' But Jesus could see how sad and worried most of those people were. They had come to him because **no one else would help**; he couldn't just turn them away. Soon he was talking to everyone, **cheering** them all up and **healing** the sick.

By evening the little boy was still clutching his picnic basket, but the stories Jesus had told were so **exciting** he had still **forgotten** to eat.

As he opened the lid, the bread and fish smelt good, but he couldn't help wondering

if Jesus had anything for his supper.

'He looks so **tired and hungry**,' thought the boy, and closing the lid again he crept towards the disciples.

'Come **on**, Master,' they were saying crossly.

'Send the people away so we can have our holiday.'

'But they're hungry,' said Jesus. 'They rushed here so quickly, most of them forgot to bring any food. It's a long walk to the shops and the children are tired.

We must give them something before they go.'

'Two hundred silver pieces wouldn't feed them all!' protested Philip, who knew they had **no** money left.

'There's a **boy** here,' said Andrew. 'He says he wants you to have his picnic, Lord. Look!

**Five** rolls and **two** fish. At least **you** won't be hungry.'

Jesus bent down and took the basket from the boy, who **never, ever forgot** the way Jesus smiled as he said,

'Thank you.'

'Tell everyone to sit down on the grass,' said Jesus and, after he had thanked God, he opened the basket and began producing fish, tucked inside the bread rolls.

'One, two…ten, eleven…twenty,…thirty!' counted the boy.

'Whatever's happening?
Jesus is bringing enough food out of my basket
to feed **everyone!** Yet I only had enough
for myself!'

As the happy, well-fed crowds walked home under the stars that night, the little boy knew that

all he ever wanted to do was to follow Jesus.

Matthew 14:1–12;
Mark 6:30–42;
John 6:8–13;
Matthew 9:36